G000152928

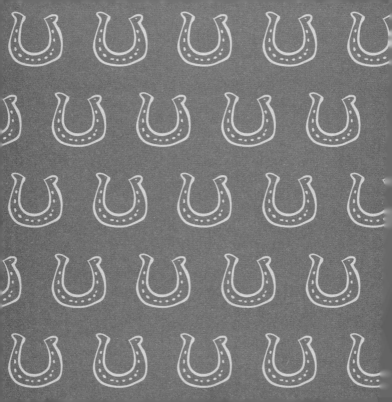

# You Know You're a
# Horse Lover
## When...

Jane Brook

Illustrations by Roger Penwill

summersdale

YOU KNOW YOU'RE A HORSE LOVER WHEN...

Summersdale Publishers Ltd
46 West Street
Chichester
West Sussex
PO19 1RP
UK

www.summersdale.com

Printed and bound in China

ISBN: 978-1-84953-166-5

Substantial discounts on bulk quantities of Summersdale books are available to corporations, professional associations and other organisations. For details contact Summersdale Publishers by telephone: +44 (0) 1243 771107, fax: +44 (0) 1243 786300 or email: nicky@summersdale.com.

To..............................................

From..........................................

Your new 'hair extensions' are actually bits of hay.

You think 'my kingdom for a horse' sounds like a good deal.

Getting new shoes means a trip to the blacksmith's, not the local shopping mall.

You insist on doing the school run on horseback.

You think being described as 'horsey-looking' is a great compliment.

You were (and still are) a member of the Black Beauty Fan Club.

You use horse-whispering techniques to reduce your horse's stress levels after a hard day's riding.

Your favourite after-dinner
palate cleanser is a salt lick.

You equate all celebrities to breeds of horses: Brad Pitt (Lipizzaner), Sarah Jessica Parker (American Spotted Donkey).

You find nothing kinky in whips, spurs and tight-fitting trousers.

Your phone's ringtone is what you'd describe as your horse 'singing.'

You shunned horsey toys as a child because they were anatomically inaccurate.

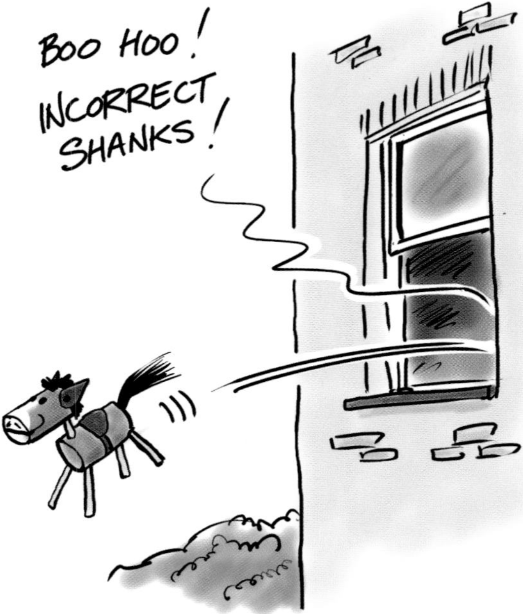
BOO HOO!
INCORRECT SHANKS!

Your bedroom looks like a
bomb's hit it, but your horse's
stall is spotless.

Your friends have all given up buying you regular birthday presents and now you only receive industrial-sized boxes of sugar cubes.

You insist on exchanging horseshoes, not wedding rings, on your big day.

The loading cursor on your computer is a tiny horse running... and this entertains you for hours.

You'd never find time to read *War and Peace* – no, your idea of 'light reading' is a 3,000-page book on horse psychology.

You never get tired of the classic 'Horse walks into a bar' joke.

You can no longer run, you either trot, canter or gallop.

You feel no need to shower after a day's riding because your horse has ever-so-kindly licked you clean.

You're regularly mistaken for a homeless person as you wait by the back door of the local grocer's to beg for leftover apples.

You're offended by hair clogging the shower drain, but laugh nonchalantly at the horse slobber, hair and chewed-up bits of carrot you pick off your riding clothes.

You have a chair in the living room especially for when your horse wants to watch the Cheltenham Festival.

You are master of the equine-themed property game Horse-opoly.

You spend hours going over the clause in your will which deals with the provisions for your horse – how else will they know about his fear of raisins?

You decide it's the end of the road for your relationship after your partner switches off *Adventures of the Black Stallion.*

You happily spend your evening baking
horseshoe cookies, but have no idea
how to even start cooking a
Sunday roast.

You encourage your partner to grow their hair so that you have something to groom while you're away from your precious.

You sent countless letters to Channel 4 asking them to take *Smack the Pony* off air, as you felt it constituted animal cruelty.

You buy coconuts specifically to cut in half and make the 'clip-clop' noise.

You invite all your house guests to ride the carousel you had installed in your back garden.

You have muscles in your thighs that nobody else knew existed.

You have trouble explaining the strange whinnying noises you make in your sleep.

You put your partner in a
halter or a bit when they get
out of hand.

You are unable to give lifts to friends as your car is stacked to the brim with spare tack and hay bales.

You kit your horse's stable out with an extra-strong, horse-sized bean bag so it can sleep in absolute comfort.

You feel an overwhelming urge to use
your riding crop to speed up the line in
the supermarket.

Your horse's toothbrush stands next to yours in the holder.

You only buy clothes which
will complement your
horse's colouring.

You tell people your height
in hands.

You use the phrase 'Whoa, Nelly!' more than ten times a day.

You keep a curl of your horse's mane in
a locket around your neck.

You belong to an online dating
site for horse lovers...

... but never have the time to log into it as you're too busy knitting your horse new leg warmers.

You look sadly at golf courses and
stately manor grounds and think,
'What a waste of nice pasture land.'

You happily forgive your horse for throwing you at the sight of a particularly scary leaf, but won't let your partner back in the house for stepping on your toe.

You post a video entitled
'Shergar: Simply the Best'
on YouTube.

You listen to 'Wild Horses' thinking sorrowfully, 'Yes, they CAN drag you away...'

Your work colleagues start thinking your new horse Nelson is actually a hunky new boyfriend, after you refer to him as your 'handsome stallion'.

You have a constant battle in your head trying to decide which is the greatest film of all time: *My Friend Flicka* or *Seabiscuit*.

While watching westerns you can't resist the urge to analyse the main character's riding style and shout, 'RELAX into the fall; no, you're doing it wrong!'

You're always in riding boots
or wellies, even at the beach.

You find yourself thinking what
nice jumps the roadwork signs would
make as you pass them in your car.

Your horoscope says you are stubborn
as a mule, and continually champing
at the bit. But unless it's straight from
the horse's mouth, you won't believe it...

You adorn your pony with a crown
after tracing his lineage back to Prince
Bedouin the Majestic of Arabia.

You can't understand why none of your friends have shown any interest in reading your show horse's 10,000-word biography *Brian: From Stable to Stage.*

You think at least one of the 17 Oscars for *The Lord of the Rings* Trilogy should have gone to Shadowfax, Asfaloth or Bill the Pony.

The only item you still own from your childhood is a rocking horse.

You run a successful online shop called Pimp My Trailer, selling home-made horse trailer accessories and decorations.

You have been banned from all the McDonalds Drive-Thrus in the area as they claim riding a horse up to the window 'is against health and safety regulations'.

Your idea of a fun night out is
spending the evening as the rear end
of a pantomime horse.

You still dream that one day
archaeologists will find proof
that Pegasus was real.

You practise your horse commands by getting your friends' kids to walk, trot or canter around the living room.

Your favourite pubs are
The Nag's Head and
The White Horse.

You gladly pass up your annual holiday to send your horse on a weekend retreat at an exclusive equine beauty spa.

Every item of clothing in your wardrobe has a horsey motif.

You're seemingly the only person in the country who knows the whereabouts of The Oat and Hay Museum.

You have 'Eau de Stable'
air freshener.

You're tempted by an advert that offers a course on 'How to interpret your horse's gurns in three easy steps'.

You can't remember family birthdays, but on the anniversary of your first dressage win you bake a cake and toast the happy occasion with carrot juice in the stable.

You force your children to watch your
*Lone Ranger* DVDs instead of
*In the Night Garden.*

You laughed yourself 'hoarse' at all this – and know your friends will too!

www.summersdale.com